AMERICAN HUMANE

Protecting Children & Animals Since 1877

Beginning Pet Care
WITH AMERICAN HUMANE

Learning to Care for
FISH

Bailey Books
an imprint of
Enslow Publishers, Inc.
40 Industrial Road
Box 398
Berkeley Heights, NJ 07922
USA
http://www.enslow.com

Felicia Lowenstein Niven

AMERICAN HUMANE

Protecting Children & Animals Since 1877

Founded in 1877, the American Humane Association is the only national organization dedicated to protecting both children and animals. Through a network of child and animal protection agencies and individuals, American Humane develops policies, legislation, curricula, and training programs — and takes action — to protect children and animals from abuse, neglect, and exploitation. To learn how you can support American Humane's vision of a nation where no child or animal will ever be a victim of abuse or neglect, visit www.americanhumane. org, phone (303) 792-9900, or write to the American Humane Association at 63 Inverness Drive East, Englewood, Colorado, 80112-5117.

To our Readers:

We have done our best to make sure all Internet Addresses in this book were active and appropriate when we went to press. However, the author and the publisher have no control over and assume no liability for the material available on those Internet sites or on other Web sites they may link to. Any comments or suggestions can be sent by e-mail to comments@enslow.com or to the address on the back cover.

Every effort has been made to locate all copyright holders of material used in this book. If any errors or omissions have occurred, corrections will be made in future editions of this book.

Bailey Books, an imprint of Enslow Publishers, Inc.

Copyright © 2011 by Enslow Publishers, Inc.

Library of Congress Cataloging-in-Publication Data

Niven, Felicia Lowenstein.
  Learning to care for fish / Felicia Lowenstein Niven.
     p. cm. — (Beginning pet care with American Humane)
  Includes bibliographical references and index.
  Summary: "Readers will learn how to choose and care for fish"—Provided by publisher.
  ISBN 978-0-7660-3193-7
  1. Aquarium fishes—Juvenile literature. I. Title.
  SF457.25.N58 2011
  639.34—dc22

                                    2009026189

Printed in China

052010 Leo Paper Group, Heshan City, Guangdong, China

10 9 8 7 6 5 4 3 2 1

Illustration Credits: All animals in logo bar and boxes, Shutterstock. © Asian Art & Archaeology, Inc./Corbis, p. 9; Bill Bachman/ Photo Researchers, Inc., p. 6; © BlendImages/Alamy, p. 43; © blickwinkel/Alamy, p. 27; Doug Martin/Photo Researchers, Inc., p. 28; Francis Lepine/Animals Animals-Earth Scenes, pp. 3 (thumbnail 1), 4–5; Gregory K. Scott/Photo Researchers, Inc., pp. 3 (thumbnail 5), 32–33; ImageSourcePink/Alamy, pp. 3 (thumbnail 4), 25; © iStockphoto, p. 17; Joerg Carstensen/dpa/Landov, pp. 22–23; Mark Smith/Photo Researchers, Inc., pp. 14, 16, 20; © Maximilian Weinzierl/Alamy, pp. 3 (thumbnail 3), 13, 21; Nature's Images/Photo Researchers, Inc., p. 15; Paul Bricknell/© Dorling Kindersley Images, p. 35; Dr. Paul Zahl/Photo Researchers, Inc. p. 19; Picture Partners/Photo Researchers, Inc., pp. 3 (thumbnail 6), 40–41; Shutterstock, pp. 1, 3 (thumbnail 2), 7, 11, 24, 31, 3 © Vstock/Alamy, p. 39.

Cover Illustration: Shutterstock (goldfish).

Table of Contents

Chapter 1
Did You Know?

Quick. What color is a goldfish? If you said gold, you are right. But you are also right if you said orange, yellow, red, brown, or black. That is because there are more than a hundred different kinds of goldfish. They each have special colors and markings.

That is just one interesting fact about goldfish. There are many more. For example, did you know that goldfish can live longer than cats or dogs? That is right.

Did You Know?

Goldfish can live for twenty years—or more. The oldest-known goldfish was more than forty years old!

There are also fish that can fly. Well, it is more like gliding on top of the water. It is really something to see!

Fish are fun to watch!

Fish can help to reduce stress.

Did you know that fish have all five senses? They can see, touch, taste, smell, and hear.

Squiggle, a goldfish in London, England, reacted to the prescence of the gas man when he came over, reported the owner of the fish, Guru Kaur. "He wrapped himself in a piece of weed which he tied into a hitch," she said. "He wouldn't come out until the man had gone. I totally understood. The gas man played loud hip-hop music and walked so heavily the floor rattled."

If you would like a pet fish like Squiggle, you are not alone. Fish are the most popular pets in America. More than 12 million families own fish. There are about 158,600,000 pet fish in the United States.

That is because fish are easy pets to keep. They do not need a lot of attention. They just need food, clean water, some light, and sometimes heat.

In return, fish give us so much. They are fun and relaxing to watch. They help us to reduce stress. They make good pets for anyone of any age or ability.

Are you ready to find out more about getting a pet fish? Turn the page and read on.

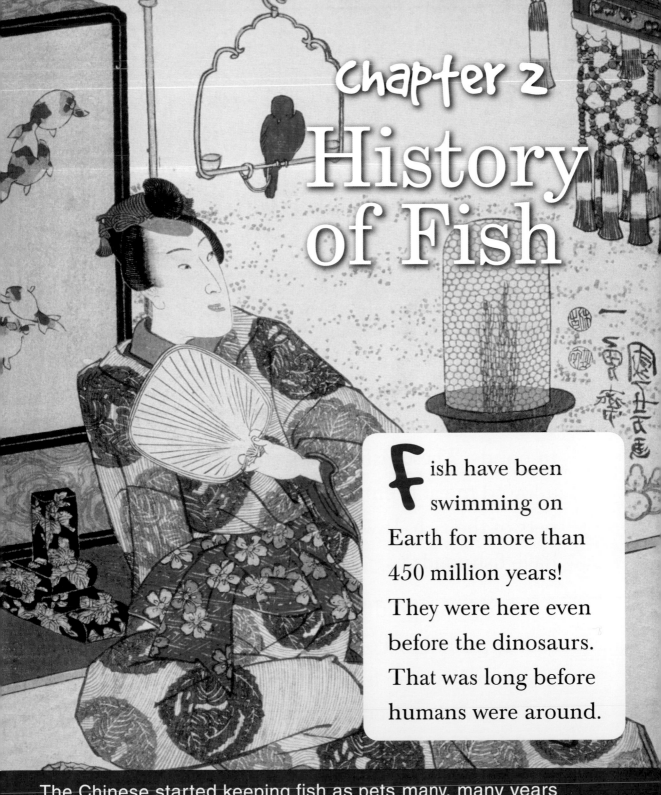

Fish have been swimming on Earth for more than 450 million years! They were here even before the dinosaurs. That was long before humans were around.

The Chinese started keeping fish as pets many, many years ago. This painting shows a man in a room with pets.

History of Fish

It seems natural that early man would have thought of fish as food. It was a little more unusual for anyone to want a fish for entertainment. But that is just what the ancient Egyptians did. They kept fish so they could look at them. They put them in containers. They worshipped certain fish. Their hieroglyphics, or picture writing, showed examples of this.

The Chinese also starting keeping fish. They bred carp and goldfish strictly as pets. They kept them in ponds. These fish were special. People were not allowed to eat them. By 1510, fish were no longer pets of the rich. It was very common for homes to have fishponds.

In 1691, the goldfish made its way to Europe. It first appeared in Portugal, then later in England. That is where the first aquarium would be built—almost two hundred years later. In the early 1800s, a man named Robert Warrington developed the first glass tank. That led to the first public aquarium at the London Zoological Gardens in 1853.

Just three years later, a German named Emil Robmaber wrote an essay called "Sea in a Glass." It talked about keeping fish as a hobby. This was a brand-new idea that started to really catch on.

At the time, pet fish were kept in tanks. The tanks were heated by gas-burning lamps, or open flames.

Today, many people visit aquariums. Aquariums are a great way to see all types of fish and other water animals.

History of Fish

This posed a problem. Sometimes the water got too hot. Other times, things caught on fire.

There were other problems with this hobby, too. People did not understand what needed to be in the water. They did not know a lot about a healthy fish diet. There was no information about the proper care of fish. So fish got sick and often died.

Over time, scientists studied fish. They learned about what fish eat. They learned how much light they needed and the best water conditions. Technology improved, too. The invention of electricity helped create heaters without flames. It became easier to keep fish as pets.

Today, we know much more about the care of fish. We also have plenty of choices when it comes to types of fish and supplies. But one thing is certain. We still enjoy keeping fish every bit as much as the ancient Egyptians.

Chapter 3
Ready to Dive In?

There are many different types of fish. They come in lots of colors and sizes. You already know about goldfish. Some other popular kinds of fish are tetras, guppies, bettas, and mollies.

Goldfish

Clownfish

Some fish live in freshwater. Others need salt water. You cannot have freshwater and saltwater fish in the same tank. That is the first decision you need to make. Will you have saltwater or freshwater fish?

Goldfish are freshwater fish. Clownfish are saltwater fish. Saltwater fish are usually more colorful. The huge tanks at many dentists' or doctors' offices are often saltwater tanks.

14

Ready to Dive In?

You may want to start with freshwater fish. It is a little easier to care for them. It is also less expensive.

You can spend a lot of money to keep fish, but you do not have to. Goldfish and guppies usually cost less than five dollars each. A ten-gallon aquarium could cost from ten to thirty dollars. People spend about one hundred dollars to start up a freshwater aquarium.

Cardinal tetras

Dalmatian molly

Saltwater fish are more expensive. A small clownfish can cost up to twenty-five dollars. You also need more supplies. You will spend at least two hundred dollars more to set up a saltwater aquarium.

Many people who buy fish do not just buy one. They buy several. How many fish will you buy? A general rule is three gallons of water for every inch of fish. So a thirty-gallon tank could hold ten one-inch fish.

Ready to Dive In?

However, the gravel and plants also take up space. Look at the space that is left. The more room you can give the fish, the better. You may want five or six fish in a thirty-gallon tank with gravel and decorations.

GRAVEL

Gravel at the bottom of a fish tank takes up space. Make sure to figure that in when you are ready to buy your fish.

Ready to Dive In?

The next decision is what kind of fish to buy. Do you want all of the same kind? Or do you want different types?

Some fish like to be with their own kind. Others fight with their own kind. They are better with other types of fish.

Neon tetras, white cloud mountain minnows, and fancy guppies are fish that get along. Male betta fish do not get along. They will want to fight. But a male betta can get along with swordtails, platies, and mollies. You can find out about which fish are best together at your local library or pet store.

Once you get your fish home, be prepared. Sometimes fish die. This can happen within the first few days. The fish could have been sick when you bought it and you did not know.

Learn from that experience. Try to choose healthy fish. These are fish that have smooth skin and

Guppies

Siamese fighting fish, or betta

bright eyes. Healthy fish swim steadily around the tank.

Also make sure you set up your home tank to keep the fish healthy. The next chapter will tell you how.

Remember that you can always ask questions if you are unsure about what to do. Pet store employees often know a lot about fish. Also, a small number of veterinarians work with fish.

Check with your local vet. If he or she does not treat fish, the vet may know about a fish club. The vet may also know an ichthyologist, a person who studies fish for a living. All of these sources are great places to find out more about fish.

Plants in a fish tank give the fish some hiding places. Ask at a pet store which are the best kind for your fish and fish tank.

Before you buy your fish you will need an aquarium. When you go to the pet store, look around to make sure the store is clean.

Chapter 4

A Healthy Home

Are you ready to bring your fish home? You will need to make sure you have the basic supplies.

The first is a place for your fish to live. You need an aquarium. These are tanks made of either glass or a type of strong, clear plastic.

A Healthy Home

The Siamese fighting fish, or betta, may do well in a bowl. All other fish should be in a fish tank.

A Healthy Home

If you are thinking of buying a fishbowl instead, think again. Bowls are not the best place for fish. There is less room to swim and most fishbowls cannot support the filter and air pump that are needed to keep fish healthy. Most fish do not do well in bowls. (The one exception is the Siamese fighting fish, also called a betta.)

Your new fish may come from the pet store in a bag. Follow the pet store's directions on how to introduce the fish to its new aquarium.

A Healthy Home

Once you have your tank, where will you put it? You need somewhere strong and steady. A gallon of water weighs a little over eight pounds. That means a ten-gallon tank weighs more than eighty pounds! Your tank will be pretty heavy when it is filled. It is best to get a stand made especially to hold an aquarium.

Make sure the tank is not in direct sunlight. Sunshine causes more algae to grow. You will have to clean your tank more often.

Put your fish in a place where they can have light during the day and dark at night. Lights that are turned on all the time can stress fish. They can even make them sick.

With your tank in place, you are ready to fill it. You may want to line the bottom with gravel. Use one pound for each gallon of water. Make sure to rinse the gravel completely before you put it in the tank. Gravel dust can clog your filter.

A Healthy Home

Fish like places to hide and explore. You can add real and fake plants and rocks, driftwood, and tank decorations, all of which you get from the pet store.

Now it is time to add the water. Water should have the right temperature, pH, and amount of salt and chlorine for your species of fish. A pet store can tell you what you need.

The water that you use will probably

Letting the bag float in the water will allow your new fish to get used to the water temperature in the aquarium.

Once your new aquarium is set up and your new fish are in, it is time to feed your fish!

be tap water. That is water right from your faucet. Just know that some tap water is treated with chemicals. Chemicals like chlorine and ammonia can kill fish. Therefore, you may need to buy a product to treat the water. A worker from the pet store can tell you what products you will need depending upon the type of fish you get.

Either way, you will want a filter and an air pump. A filter will trap waste and dirt and keep the water clean. An air pump will put oxygen into the water for the fish to breathe.

You also may need a heater. Heaters are necessary for tropical fish, whether they are freshwater or saltwater fish. Make sure to put your heater in after the tank is full. Then turn it on. Heaters can get very hot and could hurt you if they are turned on outside the water.

That is a long list, but that is not all. You still need food for your fish. Some fish are plant eaters. Others are meat eaters. Still others eat a combination. It is important to feed your fish the right diet. Otherwise, they could get sick. You may even have to feed different foods for each type of fish.

A Healthy Home

Also, throw away old fish food. Giving moldy food to fish can make them sick. Replace the food every two months, at least.

For saltwater or tropical fish, it may be necessary to set up the tank and run the filter for a few weeks before adding fish. This allows certain bacteria to grow. Some fish, especially saltwater species, depend on bacteria to create the right chemical balance in their water.

You will get your fish in a bag. Wait. Do not open the bag yet. You do not want to put the fish directly into the water. That could shock the fish.

Let the bag float in the water first for twenty to thirty minutes. The water temperature in the bag will become close to the temperature in the tank. You should also gradually replace some of the water in the bag with water from your tank. This helps the fish get used to possible chemical differences in the water. Then you can empty the contents of the bag into the tank.

Cover your tank with a screen or lid that fits it. This will help to keep household dust and dirt out of the tank. It will also prevent the fish from jumping out of the tank. Fish that eat insects often do this. The hatchet fish and comet goldfish are jumpers.

Now that you are all set up, you can relax for now. But you will need to know how to clean your tank. Check with a worker from the pet store to find out how often you should clean your tank and how to do it. This will depend on the size of the tank and the number and types of fish you have. Most tanks will need to have part of the water changed every two to four weeks. You may need to scrub the walls of the tank more often if algae starts to grow on them.

Be sure to watch
your fish every day.

Chapter 5

Problems and Challenges

Imagine that you were sent to a place where it was too hot or too cold—all the time. You were always hungry because you were not given the right food to eat. It was dirty all around you. Plus you could not breathe easily. There was not enough oxygen in the air.

Problems and Challenges

That is the kind of thing that can happen in aquariums. If the conditions in the tank are not right, fish may suffer. They can become sick or even die.

But what exactly could go wrong? One thing is the temperature. The water could be too hot or too cold for your type of fish. Another is the condition of the water. If there are too many fish, or the filter and air pump are not working, the water can be dirty. The good news is that you can watch for these problems before they become emergencies.

You also should keep a close eye on your fish. You can tell if a fish is sick. Is your fish swimming in a strange way? Maybe she is swimming in an unusual position or not really moving at all. Did your fish stop eating? Does she have spots or scars on her? Does she look puffy? Does she keep rubbing up against things? These are all signs of possible illness.

Problems and Challenges

You may want to quarantine a sick fish. That means to separate the fish from the other healthy ones. You can put her in a different tank, for example.

You can give your fish medicine. Usually that means medicated food or something to put in the water. Ask a veterinarian who knows fish. Sometimes your pet store can help, too. Unfortunately, medical care for fish is not as advanced as it is for dogs or cats. It is better to prevent problems before they occur.

Before you set up your new tank, it is a good idea to clean everything. Also, when you have sick fish, you may have to clean the tank. Ask your at a pet store for help.

Problems and Challenges

As a fish owner, you will want to know what other problems could happen. Here are some common ones.

New-Tank Syndrome and Old-Tank Syndrome

After fish eat food, their bodies make ammonia. This is a chemical that our bodies make, too. Our bodies send it outside in our urine. The fish send it back into the water through their gills.

New tanks must be set up just right or your fish could get sick.

Problems and Challenges

The problem is that too much ammonia can be deadly. The good news is that bacteria in the water usually "eat" the ammonia.

When you set up a new tank, sometimes there are not enough bacteria yet. That means they cannot take care of all the ammonia. It builds up to dangerous levels.

In an old tank, there could be a similar problem. Maybe there are too many fish or the water is too dirty. Then the bacteria cannot take care of it all.

You can test the water for ammonia. Then you can change part of the water each day until the ammonia level is normal.

Gas Bubble Disease

Sometimes there are too many gases in the water. This happens when cold water is heated too fast.

Problems and Challenges

The fish breathe in the extra gas. They get bubbles in their eyes and gills.

If this happens, you will need to get that gas out of the water. To do that, you need to move the water around more strongly. You can do that by adding an air pump to your tank or by carefully placing the tubes from your filter system. Your local pet store can show you how.

Ich or White Spot Disease

Tiny parasites can attack your fish. They burrow into the skin and create white spots.

That is why this is called white spot disease. It is also called ich, after the name of the parasite, Ichthyophthirius multifiliis. This disease can kill your fish. But you can treat ich with special medicine from your vet or pet store.

Problems and Challenges

Removing Dead Fish

You might sometimes need to remove a dead fish from your tank. You want to do this as soon as possible. Use a fish net to scoop out the dead fish. Place the fish in a plastic bag and throw it away or bury it. Then check the rest of your fish. Make sure they are healthy. If you think they could be sick, contact your pet store or veterinarian as soon as possible.

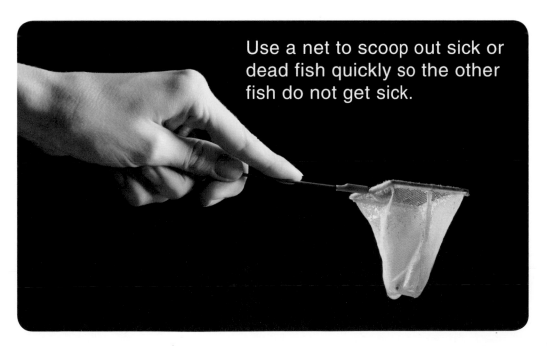

Use a net to scoop out sick or dead fish quickly so the other fish do not get sick.

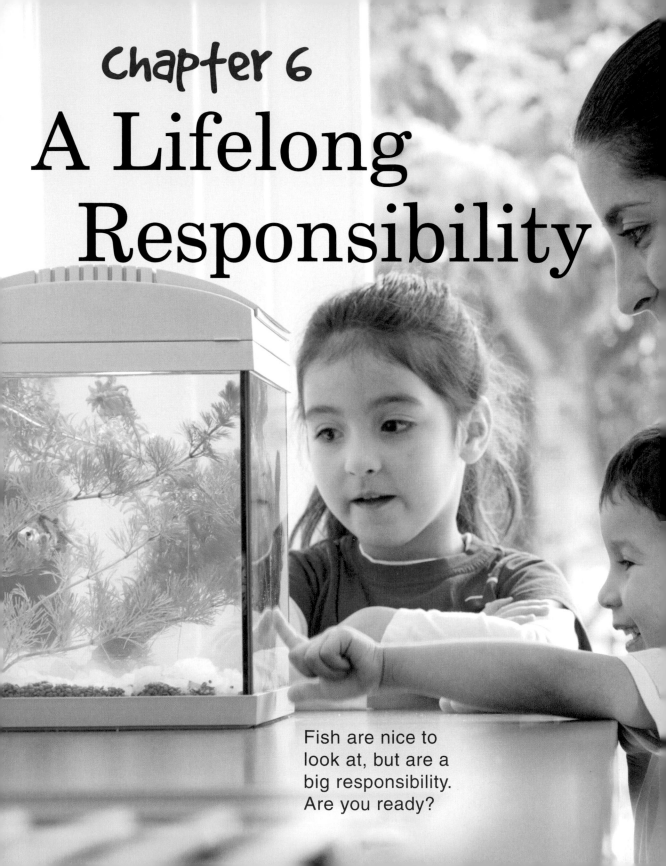

Chapter 6
A Lifelong Responsibility

Fish are nice to look at, but are a big responsibility. Are you ready?

Fish are fun to watch. Watching them helps to improve our mood. It also relaxes us. That helps reduce our stress. That is why so many doctors' and dentists' offices have fish tanks.

Fish are also beautiful. Because of that, they appear in photographs and other artwork.

"A friend talked me into getting a brilliant blue betta fish," said Beth Stafford of North Carolina. "It was like having a moving work of art. Watching Blue Max swim and flash those colors was relaxing and stimulating at the same time. I took many photos of him and did a series of abstract paintings."

A Lifelong Responsibility

Fish also make good friends for people of all ages. Take the Kim family in Florida, for example.

"I'm the one who originally wanted a fish tank filled with fish," said Ben Kim, the dad. "In Korean culture, the tradition is that having fish in your home means 'blessing.' I think I agree with this as they are quiet and soothing for me to enjoy."

"I like my fish because they boogie," said Jonathan, age five. "My fish are so hungry, like me. They like to pretend that my hand is an elevator. They go up following it."

Big brother Ian Kim, age eight, agrees. "One thing I like is that the fish in hiding come out to eat. Before I feed them every single morning, the fish act very funny!"

Karson age three, chimes in, "My fish swim in the seaweed!"

"I love the fact that they are quiet, beautiful and

A Lifelong Responsibility

therapeutic to watch and most importantly, easy for my husband to care for," said mom Karen Tinsley-Kim. "I just get to enjoy watching everyone watch each other."

You, too, can bring fish into your life and into your family. Make them a good safe and clean home, and they will entertain you for years to come.

Enjoy caring for your new fish!

Glossary

algae—A type of plant that grows in water.

aquarium—A tank filled with water, designed to hold fish.

fins—The parts of the fish that help it to swim, steer, and balance; fins almost look like wings.

freshwater—Water that is not salty.

gallon—A unit of measurement that is equal to four quarts.

gills—The parts of a fish's body that allow it to breathe oxygen underwater.

gravel—Small rocks that usually line the bottom of a fish tank.

hitch—A type of knot.

ichthyologist—A person who studies fish for a living.

Ichthyophthirius multifiliis—The name of the

parasite that causes White Spot Disease, also known as Ich.

parasite—A living thing that feeds off of another living thing.

pH—A measure of how much acid or base is in a substance, in this case water.

quarantine—Separate a sick fish from healthy ones for a period of time to reduce the spread of an illness.

salt water—Water with a high concentration of salt, similar to the ocean.

similar—Almost the same.

species—A group of fish that shares the same characteristics.

Further Reading

Books

Alderton, David. *The Encyclopedia of Aquarium and Pond Fish.* New York: DK Publishing, 2008.

Blackaby, Susan. *Fish for You: Caring for Your Fish.* Mankato, Minn.: Picture Window Books, 2006.

Buckmaster, Marjorie L. *Freshwater Fishes.* New York: Benchmark Books, 2007.

Indiviglio, Frank. *The Everything Aquarium Book: All You Need to Build the Aquarium of Your Dreams.* Cincinnati, Ohio: Adams Media, 2006.

Further Reading

Internet Addresses

American Humane Association
   <http://www.americanhumane.org>

Animal Planet: Fish Guide
   <http://animal.discovery.com/guides/fish/
   fish.html>

Index